FLY GUY PRESENTS:

POLICE OFFICERS

Tedd Arnold

Scholastic Inc.

Specially for Carter—T.A.

Thank you to the following for their contributions to this book:
AnnMarie Anderson; Officer Nicole Dillon; Detective Lennard Shulman
Deputy Inspector (Ret) Richard E. Strothman, NCPD; and
Major Latrell Simmons, Alachua County Sheriff's Office, Florida.

Special thanks to Katie Carella, who made this
Fly Guy Presents series possible, and then made it wonderful!

Photos ©: cover: H. Mark Weidman Photography/Alamy Images; back cover: David Ball/Alamy Images; 4–5: csfotoimages/iStockphoto; 6 top: Josef Prchal/Dreamstime; 6 bottom: Noah Berger/AP Images; 7 top: NoHo-Bowery Stakeholders, Inc.; 7 center: David Ball/Alamy Images; 7 bottom: Dan Callister/MEGA/Newscom; 8 top: Jpldesigns/Dreamstime; 8 center: Syracuse Newspapers/David Lassman/The Image Works; 8 bottom: Jack Foley/AP Images; 9 top: Jim West/Alamy Images; 9 bottom left: The Washington Post/Getty Images; 9 bottom right: Jochen Tack/Alamy Images; 10: Fertnig/iStockphoto; 11 top: Ringo Chiu/Getty Images; 11 center: filo/Getty Images; 11 bottom: Blue Images Online/Media Bakery; 12: Siri Stafford/Thinkstock; 12 ground: Textures.com; 13 top: Universal Images Group North America LLC/Alamy Images; 13 center: kalig/iStockphoto; 13 bottom: Mario Tama/Getty Images; 14 left: B Christopher/Alamy Images; 14 right: Luka Lajst/iStockphoto; 15: Tom Pennington/Getty Images; 16 top: stockelements/Shutterstock; 16 center: Mikael Karlsson/Alamy Images; 16 bottom: Win McNamee/Getty Images; 17 top: Thinkstock/Thinkstock; 17 center top: Marjorie Kamys Cotera/Alamy Images; 17 center bottom: avid_creative/iStockphoto; 17 bottom: kalig/iStockphoto; 18 top: tirc83/iStockphoto; 18 bottom: kaarsten/iStockphoto; 19 top left: Drew Angerer/Getty Images; 19 top right: Philip Lange/Shutterstock; 19 center: Jim Roberts/Dreamstime; 19 bottom: Knumina Studios/Shutterstock; 20 top left: Blue Images Online/Media Bakery; 20 top right: Mark Lennihan/AP Images; 20 bottom left: Saul Loeb/Getty Images; 20 bottom right: Craig Steven Thrasher/Alamy Images; 21 all: Indiana Department of Natural Resources; 21: Indiana Department of Natural Resources; 21: Indiana Department of Natural Resources; 22 top: Mario Tama/Getty Images; 22 bottom: Enigma/Alamy Images; 23 top: Rainer Jensen/AP Images; 23 bottom: a katz/Shutterstock; 24 top: Matthew Ashton-AMA/Getty Images; 24 center: ElenaBs/Alamy Images; 24 bottom: City of Granbury/Granbury Police Department; 25 top left: Marko Georgiev/Getty Images; 25 top right: Barbara Davidson/Getty Images; 25 bottom left: Image Source/Alamy Images; 25 bottom right: Huntstock/Thinkstock; 26 left: Clover No.7 Photography/Getty Images; 26 right: The Washington Post/Getty Images; 28 top: Ralph Francello/AP Images; 28 bottom: Chris Graythen/Getty Images; 29 top: Susan Stocker/AP Images; 29 bottom: Scott Olson/Getty Images; 30 top left: Dan Henry/AP Images; 30 top right: swalls/iStockphoto; 30 center left: Portland Press Herald/Getty Images; 30 bottom: Jason Getz/AP Images; 31 top: Keith Srakocic/AP Images; 31 center left: Portland Press Herald/Getty Images; 31 center right: Yi-Chin Lee/AP Images; 31 bottom: Maurice Savage/Alamy Images.

ISBN 978-1-338-21717-9

12   23

Printed in the U.S.A.   40
First printing, July 2018

Book design by Marissa Asuncion
Photo research by Emily Teresa

A boy had a pet fly named Fly Guy.
Fly Guy could say the boy's name —

Buzz and Fly Guy headed to a police station.

"We're going to meet some heroes today!" Buzz told Fly Guy.

Fly Guy put on a cape.

"Not that kind of hero, Fly Guy!" Buzz said, laughing. "Police officers are <u>real</u> heroes."

They went inside to learn more.

A police officer's job is to protect the people and property in their community. There are around 18,000 police departments in the United States.

Almost every state has a statewide police force.

Hawaii is the only state that doesn't!

A city usually has its own police department run by a police chief.

POLICE CHIEF

Large cities are broken into smaller areas, called precincts or districts. Each precinct or district has its own police station.

MAP OF NEW YORK CITY
POLICE PRECINCTS

In rural counties, there is often a sheriff's office. A sheriff oversees sheriff's deputies.

...is where the police chief or sheriff, police officers, deputies, detectives, and other staff work.

Some police stations have a locker room where officers change into their uniforms. Many also have fitness rooms.

There are often small cells to hold people who have been arrested. People stay there until they see a judge.

Some police stations have their own 9-1-1 radio operators. Other stations get information from a central 9-1-1 call center.

EMERGENCY CALL CENTERS

A law is a rule. In the United States, there are laws that say people cannot take things that don't belong to them. People also cannot go into someone's home without permission. When someone breaks these laws, they have committed a crime.

A person who sees a crime happen is called a witness.

When a crime takes place, police officers talk to witnesses to find out what happened. Then they write a report with the facts they learned.

Police officers may arrest someone when there is reason to believe that the person has broken a law.

Police officers wear uniforms. This makes them easy to spot so people know they are there to help.

HAT

RADIO

POLICE DEPARTMENT PATCH

BADGE (WITH BADGE NUMBER ON IT)

NAME TAG

SERVICE PISTOL IN HOLSTER

EXPANDABLE BATON (LOCATED BEHIND THE SERVICE PISTOL)

TASER

DUTY BELT CARRIES EQUIPMENT SUCH AS WHISTLE, KEYS, HANDCUFFS, PEPPER SPRAY, AND EXTRA AMMUNITION

STRAIGHT LEG PANTS

Most police officers wear a metal badge. Some officers, such as those on marine patrol, wear an embroidered patch.

Police officers use radios to communicate. They often use codes to let other officers know what is happening.

Police officers wear bullet-resistant vests.

lice officers do not always wear aditional uniforms while on duty.

etectives gather facts and collect hysical clues, called evidence. They work behind the scenes, so they usually wear suits or other regular clothing.

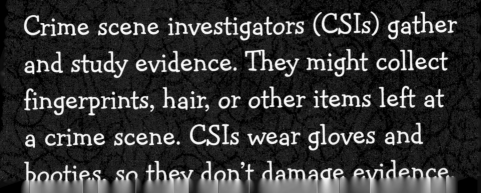

DETECTIVES

CRIME SCENE INVESTIGATORS

Crime scene investigators (CSIs) gather and study evidence. They might collect fingerprints, hair, or other items left at a crime scene. CSIs wear gloves and booties, so they don't damage evidence.

Officers on the SWAT team go through extra training, so they can handle the most dangerous jobs. They wear a special uniform to keep them safe.

SWATTERZZ?

Not fly swatters. SWAT stands for **S**pecial **W**eapons **A**nd **T**actics.

Many police officers patrol, or watch over, their communities in cars. Some police cars have special equipment inside.

Dashboard and body-worn cameras record a police officer's and the public's actions during traffic stops and arrests. The video footage can be used in court cases.

dashboard camera

body-worn camera

SAY "CHEEZZ"

Computers help an officer find out who owns a car, make sure someone's driver's license is valid, or check if a person is wanted for a crime.

Radar checks the speed of passing cars. Police officers use it to make sure drivers obey traffic laws.

Police cars have flashing lights and sirens to help keep people safe.

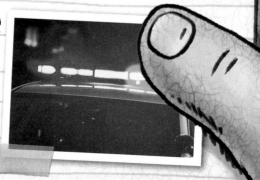

Not all police officers drive cars.

Some ride on horseback—even on city streets! Mounted officer patrols are useful in crowds since they have a better view than officers on foot.

HORSEFLYZZ!

MOUNTED POLICE OFFICERS IN TEXAS

MOUNTED POLICE OFFICERS IN NEW YORK

Others ride bicycles or motorcycles. They can reach areas a car may not be able to go.

Some police officers ride in boats. Marine patrols can help with searches and rescues in lakes, rivers, and oceans.

Police officers patrol from the sky, too. Helicopters may be used during a traffic accident or a search-

Many police departments have a Canine (K-9) Services Unit. Police dogs help police officers search people or places for drugs or weapons. They can also help track missing people.

The dogs and handlers in a K-9 unit don't just work together—they live together, too! This helps them form a tight bond.

OFFICER LEVI KNACH AND KENOBI

You're usually not allowed to pet police dogs, but don't worry. They get plenty of love!

There are around three-quarters of a million police officers in the United States. Those who want to become police officers must train at a police academy.

Trainees study local laws.

They exercise.

They learn how to use different weapons, drive safely at high speeds, and stay calm in an emergency.

After trainees graduate, they can begin active police work.

Police officers never stop learning. They continue to train and learn throughout their careers.

Police officers know how to perform basic lifesaving techniques. If people need help right away, a police officer can help.

A police officer might use the Heimlich maneuver on someone who is choking.

Or an officer might use cardiopulmonary resuscitation (CPR) on a person who isn't breathing.

A BOY THANKS OFFICER WHO SAVED HIS LIFE USING CPR

Police officers often risk their own lives to save others.

OFFICERS RESCUE WOMAN FROM FLOOD

OFFICERS INVESTIGATE CAR CRASH

HERO

OFFICER RESCUES BABY

OFFICER GIVES FIRST AID

HERO

HERO

HERO

HERO

It is important to let the police know when a crime occurs. Also, if you see a car accident or someone who needs medical help, call 9-1-1 right away!

DIZZZPATCHER!

If you call 9-1-1, the person who answers the phone will ask questions and tell you what to do until help arrives. This person is called a dispatcher.

1. Always call 9-1-1 in an emergency.

2. Tell the dispatcher your name, your location (including your street address), and your phone number.

3. Give as many details as you can about what is happening.

4. Answer the dispatcher's questions.

5. Follow any instructions, and do not hang up until you are told to.

If you dial 9-1-1 by mistake, do not hang up! Stay on the phone to let the dispatcher know you are okay.

Police officers will soon arrive at the scene. It is their job to help and to find out what happened.

Sometimes the police need help doing their job.

The National Guard is a division of the United States military. They might be called in to help the police during a natural disaster like a tornado, hurricane, or flood.

The National Guard rescues people from their homes.

The National Guard gives supplies to hurricane victims.

The United States Marshals Service (U.S.M.S.) makes sure people obey federal laws. U.S. Marshals might be called on to help the police find someone who has escaped from jail or prison.

United States Marshals escort a fugitive from the airport.

Sometimes other emergency workers—like firefighters—need help from the police.

Police officers stand guard at a roadblock so firefighters can battle wildfires.

Police officers are sworn to protect and serve their communities.

KIDS TOUR POLICE SERVICES CENTER IN TENNESSEE

OFFICERS TALK WITH A COMMUNITY MEMBER AT CALIFORNIA FARMERS MARKET

OFFICERS HELP KIDS WRAP GIFTS AT "KIDS SHOP WITH A COP" EVENT IN OREGON

A police officer might be your neighbor.

KIDS AND OFFICERS PLAY FOOTBALL IN GEORGIA

Community policing helps them do their job. That means police departments meet with community leaders and members to think about ways to solve problems before crimes occur.

FRIENDZZ!

Help keep yourself, your friends, and your family safe! If you see someone doing something he or she shouldn't be doing, tell a police officer or other responsible adult.

"Wow! Police officers have a hard job," Buzz said. "I'm glad I got to learn about so many of the things they do to help keep people safe."

Buzz and Fly Guy cannot wait until their next field trip!